بِسْمِ اللهِ الرَّحْمٰنِ الرَّحِيمِ

Muhammad, the Beloved Prophet

A Great Story Simply Told

Iqbal Ahmad Azami

UK ISLAMIC ACADEMY

ISBN 1 872531 07 5

Published by
UK Islamic Academy
147 Mere Road
Leicester
LE5 5GQ
United Kingdom

Cover design: Sultan Farooqui

British Library Cataloguing in Publication Data

A catalogue record for this book is available from the British Library.

Printed and bound in Great Britain by
DELUXE PRINTERS
245a Acton Lane,
London NW10 7NR.
Tel & AutoFax: 081-965 1771

Contents

Foreword

Islam is a universal faith and not confined to any geographical territory, race or language. More than half of the one thousand million believers in Islam in the world live in non-Arab territories. Islam, which means 'submission to the Will of Allah', is focused on the Creator's final revelations to mankind through the Prophet Muhammad, peace be upon him. These revelations are recorded in the Holy Qur'an.

Muhammad, the Beloved Prophet: A Great Story Simply Told is based on the Holy Qur'an and early sources dating back to when the Prophet was alive, 1,400 years ago. Written with young, English-speaking Muslims in mind it concentrates on the essential aspects of the Prophet's life, highlighting his excellent qualities and strength of leadership. Its 28 short chapters are aimed to encourage boys and girls to read the stories about the beloved Prophet for themselves.

The Editor hopes that this book will be useful for all those who are concerned with educating young Muslims in the English language, and that it will infuse love for the Prophet in the children's hearts. The Prophet's mission was concerned with human affairs. Understanding his mission will help to foster a shared sense of identity with all the other young Muslims in the world who are striving to be true servants of Islam.

My sincere gratitudes are due to Sister Maryam Davies, brother Jamil Quraishi and my children Muhammad, Usama and Shifa' for their assistance in producing this book. May Allah reward them all in this world and the hereafter.

Leicester, England   **Iqbal Ahmad Azami**
Rabī' al-Awwal 1411 A.H.
October 1990

5

Notes for Parents and Teachers

Please familiarise yourself with all 28 short chapters and the exercises before you start to use the book.

Only read one chapter at a time to children and leave ample time for them to answer the questions.

The stories and exercises get progressively harder so you will need to allow more time to cover work in the second half of the book.

Younger children should be able to answer the questions verbally. Remember to revise earlier stories, so that a sense of continuity is achieved and facts are memorised.

Older children should be encouraged to write the answers in sentence form in exercise books. This will enable each child to produce a useful reference book for personal use.

Children can include Arabic calligraphy and Qur'anic verses appropriate to the stories in their exercise books. In this way they will build up attractive, treasured records of their knowledge of the life of the beloved Prophet.

Notes for Children

Only read one story at a time.

When you have read a story try to answer the questions. All the answers are to be found in the stories.

Try to write your answers in an exercise book kept specially for this purpose. In this book you can also make copies of Arabic calligraphy and verses from the Qur'an.

Ask your brother or sister or a friend to read the book with you. Who can answer the most questions? Whoever knows a story best will also know more about the life of the beloved Prophet. The more we know about him the easier it is for us to try to follow his example in everything we do.

The Family Tree of the Prophet Muḥammad

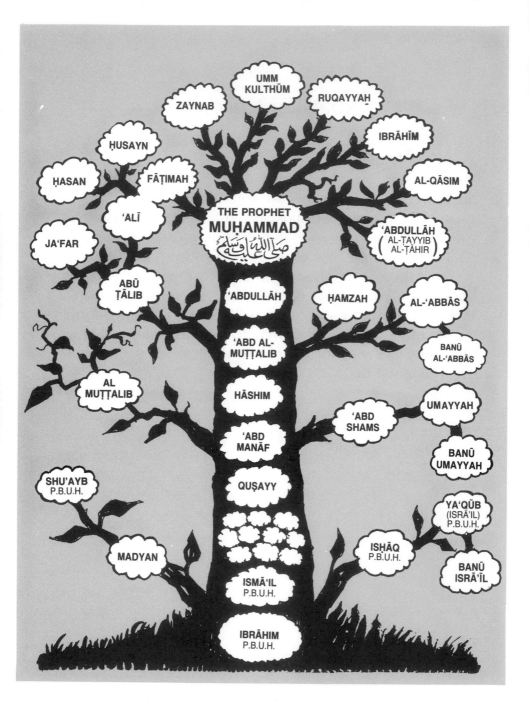

LESSON 1

The Prophet Muhammad*

The Prophet Muhammad was born in Makka, a town in Arabia, early on a Monday morning on the 12th of Rabi-al-Awwal more than 1,400 years ago. It was in the year 570 of the Christian Era (CE). That year was called Am-al-Fil or the 'Year of the Elephant'. At that time, Abraha, the Governor of Yemen, had invaded Makka intending to demolish the Ka'ba. He arrived, together with his troops, on elephants.

Abraha had set up a mock Ka'ba in Yemen **and he** wanted people to visit this one instead of the Ka'ba of **Allah** in Makka.

Allah sent flocks of birds to fly over the invaders. Each bird carried a pebble of clay. They dropped the pebbles from high up in the sky onto the invaders until all the soldiers and elephants were destroyed. Abraha fled back to Yemen, but he could not escape the wrath of Allah. Soon afterwards he died a very painful death. This story is told in the Qur'an in Sura al-Fil (105).

---

* After using the name of the Prophet Muhammad, Muslims should write or say the honorific phrase, *Salla Allahu alayhi wa sallam,* or 'Peace be upon him'. Due to limited space this honorific phrase has been omitted from both the lessons and the exercises but should be inserted when reading the book.

The Prophet's father who was called 'Abd Allah belonged to the Quraish tribe whose members were descended from the Prophet Ibrahim. 'Abd Allah died before his son's birth. The Prophet's mother's name was Amina and his grandfather's was 'Abd al-Muttalib. He was named Muhammad, by his grandfather. His mother, who had pleasing visions of him before he was born, named him Ahmad. Both names were new to the Arabs. Allah addresses him by both these names in the Qur'an.

The Prophet 'Isa (Jesus) had told his people that the most respected Messenger of Allah, whose name would be Ahmad, would come to this world after him:

> And remember, 'Isa, son of Maryam, said: 'O children of Israel! I am the Messenger of God (sent) to you, confirming the law (which came) before me, and giving glad tidings of a Messenger to come after me, whose name shall be Ahmad.'

> (Sura al-Saff 61: 6)

Exercise:

1. What was the name of the Prophet's tribe?
2. What was the day and the time of the Prophet's birth?
3. What were the names of the Prophet's parents?
4. What was the name of the Prophet's grandfather?
5. Who was Abraha?
6. Who gave the Prophet the name Muhammad?
7. Who gave him the name Ahmad?

LESSON 2

The Prophet's Infancy and Childhood

Muhammad stayed with his mother for a few days after his birth. Then, as was the Arab custom, Halima Sa'dia, a wet-nurse, took him and nursed him for two years. She was a good woman.

Halima, who had an infant son of her own, noticed that Muhammad always took his feed from the right side, leaving the left for Halima's own child. She also noticed the blessings that came with him. Her goats gave more milk than before; the rains came after a long, dry period and food which normally lasted for only two days now lasted for four.

After two years, Halima brought Muhammad back to Makka. But the city was affected by a plague so Halima, who had seen the blessings of this child, insisted on taking him back to her own village. Muhammad then stayed for a further two years with his foster-mother. He was four years old when he returned to his own mother.

When he was six, his mother, Amina, took him to visit her relatives in Madina, where they stayed for a month. Muhammad learned to swim in a pond while he was there. On the journey back to Makka, his mother died at a place called Abwa, where she was buried. Umm Aiman, who was travelling with them, took him on to Makka.

11

After his mother's death, Muhammad was brought up by his grandfather, 'Abd al-Muttalib, who loved him very much and was always happy in his company. But when Muhammad was only eight years old, his grandfather also died. He was very sad when his grandfather passed away.

After the death of his grandfather, Muhammad was taken care of by his uncle, Abu Talib. Of his eleven uncles, Abu Talib was the only real brother of his father. In his childhood, Muhammad was quite different from other children. He would never do anything mischievous nor did he quarrel with others. He liked to help his uncle. He did not take part in any of the silly games played by other children of his age.

Once he intended to visit a fair where people behaved badly. On his way he grew tired and went to sleep and he did not arrive there at all. Allah was protecting him from evil. Though idol-worship was still very common he never took part in it, even when other members of his family worshipped idols. He respected his family and co-operated with his relatives but he never joined in with them if they were doing wrong. Thus All-Mighty Allah saved him from every wrong-doing, even before his Prophethood.

One day, when Abu Talib was about to set out for Syria to trade, Muhammad asked if he could go with him. His uncle agreed and they set off together. On the way they came to a place called Busra and stopped at a Christian monastery where a monk, named Buhaira, lived. He said: 'Muhammad is the Chief of the Messengers of God.' When people asked Buhaira why he had said that, he replied that when Muhammad descended from the nearby mountain, he saw all the trees and rocks kneeling down.

Exercise:

1. Why did the Prophet feed from only one side?
2. What blessings did Muhammad bring to Halima?
3. How old was Muhammad when his grandfather, 'Abd al-Muttalib, died?
4. Why was Muhammad cared for by Abu Talib?
5. Where is Syria?
6. Buhaira was a monk. What is a monk?
7. What did Buhaira say about Muhammad?

The Prophet's Qualities and His Marriage to Khadija

Even as a young man, Muhammad had to work hard to earn a living. He looked after other people's goats, and later he gained experience of trading from his visits to Syria with his uncle Abu Talib.

His truthfulness, honesty, pleasant ways and hard work made him a successful trader. These qualities were given to him by All-Mighty Allah. He was respected throughout the land. People used to call him *Sadiq*, meaning a person who is very upright and true, and *Amin*, the trustworthy.

At one time the Quraish decided to rebuild the Ka'ba, to re-set the stones above the foundations. In one of the corners they wanted to put the black stone, but could not decide who should have the honour of placing it there. They would have quarrelled violently if the young man they all admired and trusted had not come by.

They asked Muhammad to settle the dispute. He told them to spread a large cloak and place the black stone in the middle. They did so. Then, he asked a man from each of the four clans who were in dispute to take hold of a corner of the cloak. In this way they all shared the honour of carrying the stone. When they reached the place where it was to be put, Muhammad himself took the stone and set it in the wall. This incident shows clearly how much he was respected and admired for his justice and wisdom.

Among those who came to know of the Prophet's reputation was a rich widow, named Khadija, who belonged to a merchant's family. Through some friends she approached Muhammad who agreed to handle her business affairs. Within a year of taking over Khadija's business, Muhammad had gathered together her goods for trade and set off on the journey to Syria.

Khadija had a servant, named Maisara, in whom she had great confidence. She sent him along to serve Muhammad and help with the business.

Muhammad, whom Allah had endowed with high principles and honesty did not require any supervision, however. He was able to earn more than three times the expected profit on Khadija's goods. He showed such trustworthiness and kindness that, on returning to Makka, Maisara spoke very highly of him to Khadija.

Khadija was so impressed by the account of Muhammad which her trusted servant Maisara gave to her, that, through some friends, she put her proposal of marriage to him. The Prophet accepted Khadija's proposal and they were married. Khadija was forty years old at this time and Muhammad was twenty-five.

Their marriage was a happy one and they were blessed with many children. They were respected throughout the community for their secure family life and their readiness to help others.

As the years passed by, Muhammad began to think more and more about his Creator, Allah. As his devotion to Allah increased he spent much of his time remembering

Him in the Cave of Hira, on a mountain near Makka. He usually took food with him to the cave but sometimes, when he was away from his house for a long time, Khadija would send food to him.

Exercise:

1. What are the qualities of a good trader?
2. What is meant by *Sadiq* and *Amin*?
3. Why did Khadija ask Muhammad to handle her business affairs?
4. At the time of their marriage, what was Khadija's age and how old was Muhammad?
5. Why did Khadija propose marriage to Muhammad?
6. Why did Muhammad go to the Cave of Hira?
7. Where was the Cave of Hira?

Prophethood

One day, while Muhammad was remembering his Creator in the Cave of Hira, an angel appeared before him and asked him to read. He said that he did not know how to read.

The angel pressed against his body and said: 'Read'. Muhammad replied again that he did not know how to read. The angel pressed against him and repeated his instruction. Muhammad could only reply as before. The angel then pressed against him a third time and said:

Read! in the name of thy Lord and Cherisher
Who created man
From a clot of congealed blood.
Proclaim! And thy Lord is most bountiful.
He, who taught the use of knowledge with the pen.
Taught man that which he knew not.

(Sura al-'Alaq 96: 1–5)

The Angel who brought this message from Allah was Jibril, peace be upon him, and the message was verses from the Qur'an.

The Angel Jibril appeared to Muhammad on the 17th day of Ramadan (August, 610 CE). According to the lunar calendar, he was then forty years old. This was the day when Allah bestowed Prophethood on him. For the previous six months, Muhammad was being taught by Allah through his visions. The more he remembered how the angel Jibril had brought Allah's message to him, the more his heart quivered. When he reached his house from the Cave of Hira, his heart was pounding and he was trembling all over.

While Khadija comforted him, he told her what had happened. He was worried about the great responsibility All-Mighty Allah had given him.

Khadija knew that so virtuous a man as Muhammad, her husband for fifteen years, could not be affected by anything evil. She consoled him, recalling his good deeds, how he was always kind and sympathetic to everyone, helping the needy and supporting the poor. So the good wishes of all the people were with Muhammad, and Allah showers His mercy on such people.

Khadija said to Muhammad: 'Do not be worried. You are true. You belong to Allah and Allah is with you.'

Khadija knew of an old man in Makka who was very pious and had a great knowledge of books. She felt sure he would be able to advise them about her husband's experience in the cave. Muhammad and Khadija went to this man, whose name was Waraqa bin Naufal, to tell him what had happened. Waraqa said that indeed Prophethood had been bestowed by All-Mighty Allah upon Muhammad. He added that people would mock him, but Allah would assist him and those who are virtuous would follow him.

All-Mighty Allah had chosen the best of human beings and had already prepared him to be worthy of this great mission. He had endowed him since birth with the best qualities that any human being could ever possess.

Exercise:

1. How old was Muhammad when Prophethood was bestowed on him?
2. What was the day and date when it happened?
3. Which angel appeared to Muhammad in the Cave of Hira?
4. What did the angel say to Muhammad?
5. What was the first message of Allah?
6. How had All-Mighty Allah prepared the Prophet to receive His message?
7. Why did the Prophet seek Waraqa's advice?

LESSON 5

The First Muslims

Khadija, may Allah be pleased with her, was very happy and she offered thanks to Allah for choosing Muhammad as His Prophet. As the wife of the Prophet, she understood the great honour given to her by Allah and gave thanks for that, too. In addition to being the devoted wife of the Prophet, she had the honour to become the first to believe in his Prophethood. She was the first Muslim among adult females.

Abu Bakr was an old and trusted friend of Muhammad. When he heard about the revelation, he at once expressed his firm belief in his friend's Prophethood. He knew how true, kind and gentle Muhammad was, and he had always liked and trusted him for his gracious qualities. When he learned about his Prophethood he thought it was in keeping with the virtues of the man. He became the first Muslim among adult males.

Umm Aiman, who had looked after Muhammad since his childhood, who had travelled with him to Makka after his mother's death, and had great affection for him, became the first Muslim among maidservants.

Zaid, the slave of Khadija, whom she offered to Muhammad on their marriage, became the first Muslim among slaves. The Prophet later freed Zaid and referred to him as his son.

20

A cousin of Muhammad's was 'Ali, the son of Abu Talib. He became a Muslim when he came to know of Muhammad's Prophethood. 'Ali was only ten years of age but he had great love and affection for Muhammad. He was the first Muslim among youngsters. May Allah be pleased with them all.

These first five Muslims lived close to the Prophet and shared in his daily life. They already believed that Allah was the Creator of the universe, but now, after the Prophet told them about the incident at the Cave of Hira, they said they also believed that he was the Prophet of Allah. They all made greater efforts to remember Allah and began praying to Him with more devotion.

They believed that every man should have faith in Allah, His Prophet and His Revelations. They also believed that only those who had faith would reach Salvation and those without faith would be punished by Allah. They were anxious that their friends and relatives should also know the truth so they quickly passed on the good news to them. Their relatives and friends who embraced Islam spread the news too, in their turn. For about two years Islam was spread in this way. During this time, there was no serious opposition to Islam because it was the faith of trusted relatives and close friends.

Exercise:

1. Why did Khadija become all the more devoted to Muhammad after his Prophethood?
2. Who were the first Muslims?
3. Who was Abu Bakr?
4. Who was Umm Aiman?
5. Who was 'Ali and who was Zaid?
6. Who was the first slave to become Muslim?
7. How old was 'Ali when he embraced Islam?

The Sermon on Mount Safa

Two years after his Prophethood, Allah directed the Prophet through His revelations to preach among his tribesmen that there is only One God, Allah, and that no one shares His Divinity.

The Prophet went to Mount Safa, situated in the centre of Makka, a short distance from the Ka'ba. He called for his tribesmen and when they had assembled, he said: 'If I tell you that beyond this mountain there is an army which is going to invade you, will you believe it to be true or untrue?' They all said: 'We will believe it to be true since you have always spoken the truth.'

The Prophet then said: 'I tell you that the army of death is after you. I warn you of the wrath of Allah. I am His Prophet. You should accept this as true and believe it forthwith. Stop worshipping idols. Worship Allah. Obey His commands. Reject bad actions and turn from them so that you may attain Salvation.'

On hearing this the tribesmen became angry. They worshipped many idols and even kept some of them in the Ka'ba. People from all over Arabia and beyond came to the Ka'ba to lay their offerings before these idols, and the tribesmen took these offerings for their own use. They were caretakers of the Ka'ba, custodians of the idols, and it brought them a good income. The Prophet was now asking them to give up their way of life with all its advantages.

An uncle of the Prophet, Abu Lahab, cried loudly: 'O Muhammad, have you called us here for only this?' Many of his tribesmen then deserted the Prophet.

Exercise:

1. What did the Prophet say at Mount Safa?
2. Where is Mount Safa situated?
3. To whom did the Prophet first convey Allah's message?
4. Why were the Makkans angry when they heard the Prophet's sermon?
5. Besides believing in Allah, what else should Muslims believe?
6. What is Salvation?
7. Who was Abu Lahab?

LESSON 7

Humiliation of the Early Muslims

When the Prophet spoke on Mount Safa many good people were listening. But those leaders who in their hearts worshipped idols and clung to their evil ways became angry when they heard him. They believed that he was threatening their leadership. They turned against the Prophet and his Companions, who were still very few in number. They made the Muslims' lives very miserable. They threw down thorns in their path and pelted them with dirt from the rooftops. They often beat them fiercely as well.

Arabs, since before the Prophethood of Muhammad, had always held the Ka'ba to be the House of Allah and a place for the whole of mankind. Even animals were not teased or killed near the Ka'ba. But when the Prophet went there to offer his Prayers, the non-believers tortured him. Once they put a rope around his neck when he was praying and choked him; another time they put a camel's messy intestines on his back.

The non-Muslims tried many times to murder the Prophet. Once they attacked him near the Ka'ba. Harith ibn Abi Hala, Khadija's son, who witnessed the attack rushed to defend the Prophet. He was struck down by a sword blow and died on the spot. He was the first martyr to die for the sake of Islam.

Arabia has an extremely hot climate. When the sun burns the desert sand, it is difficult to walk on it. The non-Muslims tortured the Muslims by making them lie on their bare backs on this scorching sand at midday. Then they put heavy stones on their bodies so that they could not move.

When a believer in Allah named Khabbab embraced Islam, the non-Muslims put him on a bed of hot charcoal and one of them stood on his chest so that he could not move. The scars on his body were visible for the rest of his life.

Another Muslim called Bilal was laid on scorching sand at noon and a heavy stone was placed on his chest, but he continued to say *'La-ilaha-Illa-Allah'* (There is no god but Allah). Then, the non-Muslims fastened a rope around his neck and dragged him from one end of the city to the other. Even then, Bilal continued to repeat the one word: *'Ahad'* (Allah is One). He was the *mu'adhdhin* of the Prophet and loved by all the Muslims.

Amongst the other Muslims who suffered were Ammar and his parents. His mother, Sumayya, was stabbed to death by Abu Jahl who was the Muslims' greatest enemy, while his father, Yasir, was tortured to death. Suhaib, a friend of Ammar's suffered the same treatment. When Uthman accepted Islam, he was tied up and harshly beaten by the non-Muslims including his own uncle. Abu Dhar, too, was made to lie on the ground and was severely beaten for having become a Muslim. When Zubayr declared his faith in Islam, his uncle was so angry that he tied a scorched mat around him and forced him to inhale the smoke.

The non-Muslims tormented and persecuted the Muslims in many ways. But not a single Muslim deserted Islam despite all that they suffered. This was because everyone who embraced Islam did not do it for any benefits of wealth or from fear of others, but only because of their belief in Allah.

They believed that Allah is One, and has no partner, none is His equal, He has no son, nor wife nor daughter nor brother, He exists for ever, He alone is worthy of being worshipped; to worship anyone or any thing apart from Him is the greatest sin.

They believed that pain and suffering in this world are nothing compared to the tortures of Hell. So, they obeyed Allah and His Prophet to save themselves from Hell, even though they suffered from extreme cruelty and in some cases death. Their hearts were full of love for Allah and His Prophet. They willingly endured all their difficulties and sufferings because they were Muslims.

Exercise:

1. Why did the Makkans become enemies of the Prophet and his Companions?
2. Who was Harith ibn Abi Hala, where was he killed and why?
3. What was the name of Ammar's father and what was the name of his mother?
4. Why did the Companions of the Prophet not desert Islam even when tortured?
5. What effect did the torturing of Muslims have on Islam?
6. How did Islam spread?
7. What is the object of life for a Muslim?

LESSON 8

Hamza and 'Umar Embrace Islam

In the early days of Islam, whoever became a Muslim was persecuted and ridiculed by the unbelievers. But a turning point in the history of Islam came when Hamza and 'Umar embraced Islam. Both men were very strong and brave.

One day, Abu Jahl insulted and ridiculed the Prophet Muhammad, in the compound of the Ka'ba. When Hamza heard about Abu Jahl's disgusting behaviour, he was very annoyed and went at once to the Ka'ba, where the non-Muslims of Makka were sitting. Hamza declared openly that he had accepted Muhammad as the true Prophet of Allah and that he believed in the Oneness of God. He further declared that from that day on anyone who abused Muhammad would have him to reckon with. This incident greatly encouraged the Muslims and struck a blow against those who opposed them.

Shortly after Hamza had become a Muslim, 'Umar, who had always opposed the Prophet, also embraced Islam. One day when he was still an unbeliever he was in a violent rage and he decided to kill the Prophet Muhammad. He took down his sword and strode off to attack him. On the way he met a friend who told him that his

27

sister and brother-in-law had already embraced Islam. This news made 'Umar so furious that he decided to kill his sister and brother-in-law if it were true. He set off at once for his sister's house.

On reaching the house he heard someone reciting verses from the Qur'an. He forced open the door and started beating his brother-in-law and sister, badly bruising them. In spite of 'Umar's blows they said again and again to him: 'You may kill us but we will not abandon Islam.'

'Umar understood that he could not force them to give up their belief in Islam. Impressed by their strong conviction, he asked his sister to read the verses of the Qur'an to him.

Hearing the verses changed 'Umar completely. A light of guidance came to him from Allah and he apologised to his sister and her husband for hitting them and went to find the Prophet. 'Umar went to Arqam's house where the Prophet was with his Companions and sought permission to enter. The Prophet allowed him in and asked him why he had come. 'Umar replied: 'I have come here to become a Muslim.'

Exercise:

1. Who insulted the Prophet?
2. What did Hamza do that encouraged the Muslims?
3. Why did 'Umar strike his brother-in-law and sister?
4. Who read verses of the Qur'an to 'Umar?
5. What happened to 'Umar when he heard the verses?
6. Whose house was the Prophet in?
7. What did 'Umar tell the Prophet?

LESSON 9

The Quraish Try to Prevent Islam from Spreading

After Hamza and 'Umar embraced Islam, the situation changed for the better and Islam began to flourish. The word of God, the light of guidance towards the noble path, began to reach large numbers of unbelievers more easily.

When the Quraish tribe of which the Prophet was a member saw that their attempts to prevent Islam from spreading had failed, they tried to persuade Muhammad to stop preaching Islam. They offered him all the wealth that they had. They even offered him the leadership of the tribes if he would abandon this new religion. But all their efforts were in vain.

In a last effort to persuade the Prophet to give up Islam the Quraish sent Utba ibn Rabia, a rich tribal chief to talk to him. Utba, an old man, could not, in spite of all his experience, get Muhammad to change his mind. He asked him about the message Allah had revealed to him. The Prophet recited some verses from the Qur'an and Utba listened intently.

When Utba returned to the other tribal chiefs, he reported to them: 'The message that he is preaching is not a man-made message. It is impossible to make him give up Islam.' The Quraish were disappointed when they heard this and they knew that they must find some other way to stop the Prophet.

About five years after the Prophet Muhammad had announced his Prophethood there was still opposition to him from the unbelievers. It was decided that some of the Prophet's followers should go to Habasha (Ethiopia) for safety. They could practise and preach Islam there and live in peace. This migration, for the sake of religion and in the way of Allah, is known as the *Hijra.*

The first group of devoted Muslims to migrate was made up of twelve men and two women. Among them was Uthman ibn Affan. One of the women was Ruqayya, daughter of the Prophet, who was married to Uthman.

Shortly afterwards, when another caravan, of eighty-three men and eighteen women set off for Habasha, the unbelievers tried to stop them but they still reached Habasha safely. The Quraish then sent a deputation to the King of Habasha, who was a Christian, asking him to turn the Muslims away.

The king listened patiently to the Muslims. They recited part of Sura Maryam from the Holy Qur'an for him and he was very impressed. He said: 'This that you have recited to me, and the one given to Musa, are both from the same source of light.' He then told the Muslims that they could stay and practise their religion in peace in Habasha.

The unbelievers of Makka realised that the tactics they were using against the Muslims had failed and that despite all their efforts Islam was flourishing. Then they decided to try a social boycott of the Muslim community. An agreement was prepared and signed by almost all the shopkeepers and businessmen of Makka.

They agreed not to buy anything from the Muslims or sell to them nor have any dealings with them. They decided that no one should have any social links with the Muslims, and no jobs should be offered to them. The agreement was displayed in the Ka'ba. Anyone breaking its terms would face the same social boycott as the Muslims.

Because of the boycott the Muslim community decided to move to a small valley known as She'b Abu Talib. There the Prophet and his faithful followers lived for almost three years. During this time the Muslims endured such hardships as few communities on earth have ever known but their devotion to the cause of Islam never wavered.

After three years, many of the unbelievers of Makka felt that their ill-treatment of the Muslims had gone far enough and they decided to lift the boycott. So, the long period of physical and mental agony for the Muslims eventually came to an end. The unbelievers now realised that it was impossible to make the Muslims change their religion. They knew that the Muslims were so devoted to Islam that no worldly power could change them.

Exercise:

1. How did the Quraish try to stop the Prophet from teaching Islam?
2. Why did the Quraish send Utba ibn Rabia to talk to the Prophet?
3. What did Utba tell the tribal chiefs?
4. Why did some of the Prophet's followers go to Habasha?
5. What is this migration known as?

6. How many Muslims were in the first group that migrated to Habasha?
7. Why did the unbelievers decide on a social boycott of the Muslims?
8. What form did the boycott take?
9. How long did the boycott last?

LESSON 10

The Year when Abu Talib and Khadija Passed Away

Ten years of the Prophethood of Muhammad had passed when two sad events took place. These were the death of his very dear and kind uncle, Abu Talib, and the death of one of the noblest ladies of all times, Khadija his wife.

History will always record with honour that during the times of opposition to Islam, Khadija devoted her life and all her property to the faith. She was the richest lady in Makka. And she had been the first to embrace Islam.

After Abu Talib's death, conditions became more difficult for the Muslims as it was mainly out of respect for him that the Prophet Muhammad and his followers had not been forced to leave Makka.

The deaths of Abu Talib and Khadija were a great loss to the Muslims but the Prophet bore his own grief patiently and continued his mission to take the word of Allah to the people.

At that time, seasonal get-togethers of villagers and different tribes took place at Mina near Makka. The Prophet went to these gatherings to preach the word of Allah. But his task was made difficult because the people were still

33

reluctant to give up the old beliefs. Also, Abu Lahab tried to mislead the people and ridiculed the Prophet whenever he tried to preach.

Although only a few people became Muslims the constant efforts of the Prophet meant that news about Islam reached every corner of Arabia. He had been asked by some people of Ta'if to visit them so that they could hear verses of the Qur'an and then they might embrace Islam. When the Prophet after a long journey, reached their village, some nasty people and older children threw stones at him. He was badly shaken by their sudden aggressive attack.

The Archangel Jibril appeared to the Prophet and said that he had been given permission by Allah to turn the land inhabited by the Ta'if people upside down. But the Prophet said: 'No! These people do not understand the message of Allah at present but will come to know it some time.'

On his journey home, the Prophet stopped to rest by a garden wall, where he prayed to Allah:

> O Allah, to You I complain of my weakness, helplessness and lowliness before men. O Most Merciful, You are the Lord of the weak, and You are my Lord. To whom would You leave my fate? To a stranger who insults me or to an enemy to whom You have given power over me? If You are not angry with me, I care not what happens to me. Your favour alone is my objective. I take refuge in the Light of Your countenance by which the darkness is illumined and on which this world and the other depend, lest Your anger descend upon me or Your wrath light upon me. It is for You to be satisfied until You are well-pleased. There is no power and no might save through You.

34

It so happened that Utba ibn Rabia and Shaiba ibn Rabia, who owned the garden, sent their servant to the Prophet with some grapes. Before he began to eat the grapes, the Prophet said *'Bismillah'* meaning 'In the name of Allah'. The servant, whose name was Addas, was very surprised to hear those words and said: 'This is not the way the people of this country speak.'

'From what country do you come, Addas, and what is your religion?' asked the Prophet. 'I come from the Assyrian town of Ninevah and I am of the Christian faith', he replied. 'From the same town as Yunus, the son of Matta', added the Prophet. 'How do you know of him?' asked Addas in surprise. 'He is my brother – he was a Prophet and I am a Prophet', said Muhammad. Addas then knew that this man was really a Prophet and he kissed his feet.

Later, on the same journey, the Prophet was again praying to Allah when he was overheard by some *jinn* who were close by. The *jinn* were so impressed by the Prophet's prayers that they also decided to become Muslims.

Exercise:

1. Why did things become more difficult for the Muslims after Abu Talib's death?
2. How did the Prophet face the loss of his wife Khadija?
3. How did the Prophet try to spread the word of Allah?
4. Why was his task made more difficult?
5. How did Islam eventually spread to the whole of Arabia?
6. Why did the people of Ta'if ask the Prophet to visit them?

7. Why did the Prophet ask the Archangel Jibril not to punish the people of Ta'if?
8. How did the Prophet know of Yunus, the son of Matta?
9. How did Addas know that Muhammad was truly a Prophet?

LESSON 11

The Night Journey

One night the Prophet was awoken from his sleep by the Archangel Jibril, who led him to the door of al-Masjid al-Haram where Buraq, an animal from Paradise was waiting. The Prophet mounted Buraq and, accompanied by the Archangel Jibril, was taken swiftly to the al-Aqsa Mosque in far-off Jerusalem. There the Prophet had two jugs placed before him, one containing wine and the other milk. When the Prophet chose the milk the Archangel Jibril said: 'You Muhammad, have been rightly guided to the true nature of man, and so will your people be. Wine is forbidden to you.'

The Prophet was then taken through the gates of Heaven where he saw countless angels. He was also shown a glimpse of Hell and the terrible plight of those who suffer there.

Then the Prophet was taken by the angels through the Seven Heavens and along the way he saw the Prophets 'Isa, Musa and Ibrahim. He also saw the Prophets Yahya, Yusuf, Idris and Harun.

Then he was taken into the Divine Presence of Allah, who told him that Muslims should pray fifty times each day.

On his way back through the Seven Heavens, however, the Prophet again saw Musa who asked him how many prayers the Muslims had been instructed to perform. When the Prophet told him fifty, Musa said: 'Your people are weak, they may find it difficult to pray so many times each day. Go back to your Lord and ask him to reduce the number for your community.' Muhammad did so, and Allah reduced the number by ten.

When the Prophet passed Musa again he asked the same question and again he advised him to seek Allah's permission to reduce the number of prayers. This went on until Allah said that Muslims should pray five times each day. Even then, Musa advised the Prophet to return yet again to Allah, but the Prophet said: 'I have asked the Lord to reduce the number of prayers until I am ashamed. I will not ask Him again. He who performs the five prayers faithfully will have the reward of fifty prayers.'

The next morning when he returned to Makka, the Prophet told the Quraish about his journey to the Seven Heavens. Most of them refused to believe that the Prophet had been on such a long journey in a single night.

Many Muslims were also amazed by the Prophet's story and some ran to Abu Bakr with the news. But Abu Bakr said: 'By Allah, if Muhammad has said so then it is true. Remember that the Prophet receives the word of Allah directly from Heaven at any time of the day or night. Is not that a greater miracle than what you doubt now?'

When Abu Bakr went to the mosque and heard the Prophet's description of Jerusalem, he said: 'O Prophet of Allah, you tell the truth.'

The Muslims who had earlier doubted the Prophet's story also believed him when he described two caravans he had seen on his way back to Makka, for when the caravans arrived later in Makka they were just as the Prophet had described them.

Exercise:

1. Who woke the Prophet?
2. How did the Prophet make the night journey to Jerusalem?
3. Which mosque was the Prophet taken to in Jerusalem and what happened there?
4. Whom did the Prophet meet on his journey through the Seven Heavens?
5. What did Allah tell the Prophet?
6. Why did Musa tell the Prophet to go back to Allah?
7. What did the Prophet say would be the reward of those who prayed five times each day?
8. Did everyone believe what the Prophet told them about his journey?
9. What happened to prove that he had told the truth?

LESSON 12

Islam Spreads to Madina

Yathrib, which was later called Madina (the city), is revered world-wide as the Prophet's city. It is about 300 miles from Makka. The weather in Madina is usually better than in Makka. The soil is suitable for agriculture, but because there is so little rain the crops are not very good. The people of Madina were, like the people of Makka, idol-worshippers.

The Aws and the Khazraj were two well-known tribes of Madina. They had once lived in Yemen but after a terrible cyclone they had migrated to Madina. Other tribes also lived around Madina. They were Jews whose ancestors had also migrated to Madina from other lands. Most of the Jews were businessmen and the Aws and the Khazraj were farmers and labourers.

At one time, because of a tribal disagreement, fierce fighting broke out between the Aws and the Khazraj. As a result, the Aws were defeated and most of their bravest men were killed. They then went to Makka to seek help from the Quraish. While their delegation was in Makka, the Prophet Muhammad met them and told them about Islam. When the delegation returned to Madina, they told other members of their tribe about Islam and the Prophet. In this way Islam was first introduced to the people of Madina.

Another time, a group of people from Madina came to Makka. Among them was a poet and scholar named Suwaid. When this group met the Prophet, Suwaid told him that he had a book which contained many beautiful things. However, when he heard the Prophet recite verses from the Qur'an, Suwaid admitted that they could not have been written by a man, as they contained Divine words. When this group returned to Madina, they also talked about Islam to their friends.

Ten years had passed since the first revelation when another group of six people came to Makka from Madina. They showed great interest in Islam. Upon hearing verses from the Qur'an they were convinced that it was the Word of Allah and they embraced Islam. They returned to Madina as Muslims and preachers.

The following year these six Muslims returned to Makka and brought with them another twelve people, who had already accepted Islam and believed that Muhammad was the Messenger of Allah. They embraced Islam at the hands of the Prophet who entered into an agreement with them. Their pledge was made near a hillock. As the Arabic word for hillock is "Aqaba', it is known as the Covenant of 'Aqaba.

The terms of the agreement were these:

1. None is to be worshipped but Allah.
2. No one will steal.
3. No one will kill his child, be it a girl or boy.
4. No one will put any blame on another.
5. Everyone will obey the orders of the Prophet Muhammad.
6. Everyone will try to correct social evils.

7. Everyone will practise Islam openly and no one will hide his being a Muslim because of oppression and harassment from non-Muslims.

This small group of Muslims asked if a preacher could return with them to Madina. Muhammad asked Mus'ab to go with them to preach the Word of Allah.

Mus'ab preached Islam with such dedication and devotion that, a year later when the Muslims of Madina returned to Makka to perform *Hajj*, they numbered seventy-three men and two women. After performing *Hajj*, they all declared that they were followers of the Prophet Muhammad.

Once again, they gathered near a hillock and entered into an agreement with the Prophet. This agreement is known as the second Covenant of 'Aqaba. They asked the Prophet to come to Madina so that they could benefit from his presence and his teaching. Abbas, an uncle of the Prophet, addressed this group of Muslims and asked how the Prophet would be treated if he went to Madina. They assured him that they would protect him against any harm and never betray him, even if they had to sacrifice their lives and property.

Then the Prophet selected twelve from among them to be preachers of Islam. One of the Muslims asked him what their reward would be for preaching Islam. He told them: 'The pleasure of Allah and an eternal stay in Heaven.' Hearing this, the Muslims were so overjoyed that tears appeared in their eyes.

Exercise:

1. Name three tribes who lived in Madina.

2. How was Islam introduced to the people of Madina?
3. How did Suwaid the poet know that the Qur'an was the book of Allah?
4. How did the 'Aqaba Agreement receive its name?
5. Describe four of the terms of the agreement.
6. Why did the Prophet ask Mus'ab to go to Madina?
7. Why did the Muslims want the Prophet to go to Madina?
8. Who asked if the Prophet would be treated well if he went to Madina?
9. What is the reward for preaching Islam?

LESSON 13

The Hijra

The Prophet now decided that the time had come for the Muslims of Makka to migrate to Madina, where they could live as true Muslims and preach Islam. He instructed them to leave for Madina in small groups. The Prophet would leave when his followers were safely in Madina.

When the Quraish of Makka realized that most of those who had accepted Islam had migrated to Madina, they were very angry. They decided to kill the Prophet. He was to be murdered by a group of young men, who would be chosen from different tribes so that no one tribe could be blamed for the murder.

While they plotted, Abu Bakr hired two camels and a guide for their journey to Madina. The unbelievers knew that the Prophet was soon to leave Makka. The young men who were to murder him surrounded his house during the darkest hours of the night and settled down to wait for the dawn, when they would carry out their evil plan.

In fact, the Prophet had been ordered by Allah to leave for Madina that very night. He asked 'Ali to sleep in his bed and told him that, in the morning, he should hand over to their owners all the belongings that he was taking care of for them. Although the unbelievers of Makka did not follow the Prophet's religion, and they hated Islam enough to want to kill him, they had never found him to be dishonest and they would leave their precious belongings in his safe-keeping. Now, despite all their persecution and murderous plans, the Prophet's main concern was that their property should be returned to them.

So, the Prophet left his house at midnight and, by the grace of Allah, all the young men who were surrounding the house intending to kill him did not see him leave.

In the morning when the young men rushed into the Prophet's house they were amazed to find 'Ali in the Prophet's bed. They could not understand how Muhammad had left the house without being seen. They set off to search for him in Makka.

By this time the Prophet had met Abu Bakr outside Makka and they had begun their journey to Madina. After a time they needed to rest and sought refuge in a cave known as Thaur. While they were in the cave, a miracle happened. A pigeon built its nest in a bush overhanging the mouth of the cave and a spider wove its web over the entrance. They did this so quickly that nobody would believe that the Prophet and Abu Bakr had entered the cave only a short time before.

The men from Makka who were searching for the Prophet once passed close to the cave. But, seeing the pigeon's nest and the spider's web covering the entrance, they did not look inside. The Prophet and Abu Bakr decided to stay in the safety of the cave for a few days in the hope that the young men of Makka would tire of searching for them. Asma', the eldest daughter of Abu Bakr, brought them food and a servant grazed his herd of goats close by and supplied them with milk.

In fact, the family of Abu Bakr made numerous sacrifices in the name of Allah and for the sake of Islam.

Once, one of the richest families in Makka, they became one of the poorest, but they never once thought of giving up Islam. Abu Bakr later became the first Caliph of Islam.

After the Prophet and Abu Bakr had spent three days in the cave, the two camels were brought there and the small party set off for Madina. The Prophet and Abu Bakr rode on one camel and the guide and Abu Bakr's servant rode on the other.

Back in Makka, the non-Muslims were angry that the Prophet had escaped. They offered a reward of one hundred camels for his capture. Many people set out to win the reward. One of these was Suraqa ibn Ju'sham. He hired a speedy horse and travelled so fast that he soon came within sight of the Prophet's party. But, by a miracle, when he tried to ride up to them his horse slipped and its legs became half buried in the sand. He tried a second time, and the horse stumbled again and Suraqa was hurt. He knew then that Allah was protecting the Prophet's party.

Having witnessed the power of Allah, Suraqa apologised to the Prophet for pursuing him. When he was returning to Makka, he came upon some other people heading the same way in the search. Suraqa told them to go back as he had found no trace of the Prophet.

Exercise:

1. Why did the Prophet decide the Muslims should migrate to Madina?
2. How were the Muslims to make the journey to Madina?
3. Why did the Quraish decide to kill the Prophet and how did they plan to do it so that no one tribe would be blamed?

4. Why did the young men surround the Prophet's house during the night?
5. Why did the Prophet ask 'Ali to sleep in his bed?
6. What miracle happened at the Cave of Thaur?
7. How did the Prophet and Abu Bakr receive food while they were in the cave?
8. Why did Suraqa set out in pursuit of the Prophet's party?
9. How did Allah protect the Prophet's party?

LESSON 14

The Prophet Settles in Madina

The Prophet's migration *(Hijra)* as commanded by Allah marks a turning point in the history of Islam. The Islamic calendar is based on this event. The year consists of twelve months, starting with Muharram and ending with Dhu al-Hijja.

News that the Prophet had left Makka spread throughout Madina. Muslims there looked forward to his arrival. Every day they gathered at the town gates to welcome him. It was on a Monday afternoon, 12th Rabi al-Awwal that a Jew, who was working at the top of a fort, saw the Prophet's party approaching the town.

The Prophet, clad in white, was riding a camel. The Jew shouted: 'O people, here is the one you have been waiting for.' The news filled the Muslims with great joy. They dressed in their best clothes. The men put on armour and drew their swords, as was their custom for receiving a noble person. Then they made their way to Harra, on the outskirts of Madina, to welcome the Prophet.

As the Prophet and Abu Bakr entered the town, the waiting Muslims' joy knew no bounds. It was the best day of their lives.

The Prophet spent a few days at Quba, a small

village three miles from the entrance to Madina. Kulthum ibn Hadm, chief of the Aws, had the privilege of being his host. The Prophet laid the foundation stone of a mosque in Quba which Abu Bakr, 'Umar and other Companions helped to build.

It was on a Friday that the Prophet and Abu Bakr set out for Madina. When they reached Bani Salim, it was time for the Midday Prayer. The Prophet offered the prayer and delivered the sermon *(khutba)*. This was the first Friday Congregational Prayer with a sermon in the history of Islam.

All the Muslims were full of joy. Madina was crowded with the Prophet's devoted followers. Women watched the scene from the rooftops of their houses while the children took an active part in the welcome. Young girls sang in praise of him and everyone welcomed him warmly. Almost everyone asked the Prophet to be their guest. To decide the matter, the Prophet said that he would stay wherever his she-camel, Qaswa, knelt down. The Prophet knew that Allah would guide his camel to stop at a suitable place.

Finally the camel stopped in the locality of Bani al-Najjar, the tribe to which the Prophet's mother had belonged.

The piece of land belonged to two young orphans, Sahl and Suhayl. The Prophet decided to build a mosque and his own rooms there. The two brothers wanted to give the land to the Prophet as a gift, but he insisted on paying them for it.

The Prophet laid the foundations of the mosque, then he, his Companions and many willing helpers completed the rest of the building. The walls were of mud and stone and the pillars of palm. Two rooms were also built at one side of the mosque. They were very small and the ceilings were very low. Until they were ready, the Prophet was the guest of Abu Ayyub al-Ansari, who was delighted to have the Prophet stay in his house.

The Prophet now turned his attention to the affairs of the Muslim community. Many Muslims had migrated to Madina and the community was made up of the *Muhajirun* (Emigrants) who had come from Makka, and the *Ansar* (Helpers) who lived in Madina.

The Prophet knew that the newcomers to Madina needed to be able to earn their own living so that they could settle down quickly. He told the *Ansar*: 'These *Muhajirun* are your brothers in faith. You should treat them as your own brothers.' The *Ansar* readily agreed to the Prophet's proposal. Each of them accepted a *Muhajir* as his brother, took him into his house and offered him half of all his belongings.

It was a gesture of great sacrifice on the part of the *Ansar*. The *Muhajirun* were overwhelmed by such generosity and brotherly love. Because of this help they were soon able to earn their own living and repay their *Ansar* brothers.

Exercise:

1. How far is Quba from Madina?
2. How long did the Prophet stay in Quba?
3. How did the Prophet decide where he should stay in Madina?
4. How was the Prophet's mosque built?
5. To whom did the land belong on which the Prophet built his mosque?
6. What was the need for establishing this brotherhood?
7. How was it practised?
8. Who were the *Ansar* and who were the *Muhajirun*?
9. How did the *Ansar* help the *Muhajirun*?

50

The Battle of Badr

The Qur'an describes the Prophet Muhammad as the 'Mercy for all the worlds'. Islam preaches peace and friendly relations among the followers of different faiths. Though the Muslims were severely persecuted, they never tried to harm their oppressors. Instead, they prayed for their guidance. These features, unique to Islam, were seen in the life of Muslims in Madina. First, the Prophet brought to an end the centuries-old feud between the Aws and Khazraj, the two leading tribes in Madina. They joined together in an Islamic brotherhood.

So that the Muslims and Jews in Madina could live in peace together, the Prophet made an agreement with the Jews that both peoples should be free to practise their own faith. They would jointly help anyone who was oppressed. They would treat each other with respect and friendliness and fight together against any common enemy. It was also agreed that in any dispute the Prophet's decision would be final.

The Jewish community in Madina was made up of three leading tribes: Bani Nadir, Bani Quraiza and Bani Qainuqa. Each of them was a party to this pact. The Prophet also made similar pacts with other tribes in and around Madina.

Though the Makkan Quraish had failed in their

attempts to check the spread of Islam and to stop the Prophet from migrating to Madina, they had not given up their fight. They now tried to force the Aws and Khazraj tribes to fight against the Muslims and threatened them if they did not agree. As most members of these tribes had already embraced Islam, however, they would not fight the Muslims. Angered by this, the Quraish banned all Muslims from Makka. As it was a holy city it should have been open to all.

The Quraish made a similar threat against the Jews of Madina. They also planned to get rid of the Prophet and chose Umair, a Makkan, to kill him, but Umair refused.

The Quraish prepared for war against the Muslims, too. They levied a tax on all Makkans and invested the money collected in trade so that it grew into a large sum to fund the fighting. Abu Sufyan led a trade caravan to Syria to help boost the war funds. On the journey back to Makka, he raised a false alarm. He called for the Quraish to help defend the caravan against a Muslim raid. The Quraish had been looking for an excuse to wage war against the Muslims so, as soon as they received the message from Abu Sufyan, they marched out of Makka in great strength. They were confident of defeating the Muslims. The Quraish army, drawn from all the leading tribes, numbered almost 1,000 well-equipped men.

As the chief of Madina, it was the Prophet's duty to protect not only the Muslims but also the Jews with whom the Muslims had entered into an agreement. When he learned of the approaching caravan headed by Abu Sufyan, he directed a raid on it, for it posed a serious threat to the Muslim community. His Companions, ever ready to obey the Prophet's commands, joined the raid expedition. They reached Badr, a place eighty miles from Madina through which all the trade caravans used to pass.

Abu Sufyan, realising that the Muslims were coming, had taken another route. The Prophet and his Companions were surprised to find themselves facing the huge Quraish army. They had only intended to raid Abu Sufyan's trade caravan. They were not equipped for battle. They numbered only 313, including a number of young boys. They had only a few weapons and just two horses and seventy camels.

The Prophet held a council to see how the Muslims felt about the turn of events. The *Ansar,* who were pledged to help the Prophet and his Companions if they were attacked in Madina, now found themselves facing a new situation. The Prophet asked them what they thought should be done. The *Ansar* at once agreed to support the Prophet. They began to prepare for battle against the mighty Quraish army. The *Muhajirun,* the Muslim migrants from Makka, were also keen to fight back.

The *Ansar* chief then made a moving speech in which he said: 'O Messenger of Allah! The moment you direct us to fight, we will be the first to do so. We are willing to go to any lengths to obey your command. We are not like the companions of Musa, who told the Prophet to fight the enemy alone. We will follow you at all times.' His brave words were welcomed by the Prophet and encouraged the small force of Muslims who now made ready to face the Quraish.

Even while making preparations for battle the Prophet set an example of fair conduct. Two Muslims on their way back to Madina had been captured by the non-Muslims. They had been allowed to go free on condition that they did not take part in the battle. When they reached the Muslims, the Prophet ordered them to stay out of the battle, despite the need for every available man to help.

53

As the battle began, the Prophet offered the following prayer: 'O Allah! If these handful of Your slaves perish today, there will be none, till the Last Day, to worship You.' Although the Prophet was assured of Divine help, he constantly prayed to Allah.

In the battle which took place on Friday, 17th Ramadan, Allah granted the Muslims Divine help. He gave them courage and confidence. He also sent down rain the night before the battle to help the Muslims. The area over which they had to march was very sandy, but when it rained, the ground became firm and they were able to keep their feet better on their part of the battlefield. The rain, however, fell much heavier on the Quraish side. The whole area became marshy which slowed down their movements.

The Muslims fought so well that the Quraish suffered a heavy defeat. Among their chiefs Abu Jahl, 'Utba, Shaiba and Umayya ibn Khalaf were killed and seventy Quraish were taken prisoner. Although the Prophet's own uncle Abbas and his son-in-law were among the prisoners, they did not receive any special treatment. All the captives were treated equally well. It was decided to exchange them for ransom money. Some were also released after a while because they had helped to teach the Muslim children in Madina.

The prisoners of war, in contrast to the custom of the time, were not bound or kept imprisoned. They were given into the care of several Companions, who treated them in a brotherly manner. They gave the captives food, even though they themselves had very little to eat.

When the defeated Quraish army returned to Makka, there was gloom all around. The Quraish chiefs vowed to take revenge on the Muslims and, having elected

Abu Sufyan as their leader, began preparing for another attack.

Exercise:

1. Describe the role of the Prophet in Madina.
2. What were the names of the three leading Jewish tribes in Madina?
3. What were the main conditions in the Prophet's pact with the Jews?
4. What did the Quraish plan to do to the Prophet?
5. Why was the Battle of Badr fought?
6. What was the role of the *Ansar* in the battle?
7. How strong was the Muslim army?
8. What was the outcome of the battle?
9. How were the prisoners treated?

LESSON 16

The Battle of Uhud

Eventually, Abu Sufyan led an army of 4,000 men towards Madina, determined to crush the Muslims once and for all. When the Prophet learned of the advancing army, he discussed with the Companions how best to meet this new threat. It was finally decided to face the Quraish army some distance from Madina.

The Muslim soldiers numbered barely 1,000, of whom 300 returned to Madina before the battle. They were led by Abdullah ibn Ubayy and came to be known as 'the hypocrites'. This name is given to them in the Qur'an. Hypocrites were people who pretended to have joined the Muslims but were really their enemies, just waiting for the chance to turn against them. After their leader, Abdullah ibn Ubayy, gave them the order to desert the Muslim ranks, the Muslims were left with only 700 men to fight against 4,000.

When the Prophet was choosing the men to face the Quraish, a number of young boys wanted to fight for Islam. Rafey', one of the youngsters, by standing on his toes, made himself appear taller and was selected. Samura, another young boy, then insisted on being included because he was strong enough to knock down Rafey'. When, in a contest of wrestling, Samura defeated Rafey', he was also allowed to join the Muslim force.

The Quraish army had camped by the Uhud mountain. As the mountain was behind the Muslim army, the Prophet, worried about an attack from that direction, positioned fifty archers to guard the Muslim rear.

As the battle raged, the Muslims fought so fiercely that many of the Quraish chiefs were killed. The Quraish ranks eventually broke and they began to retreat. Believing that they had won the battle, the Muslims started to collect the booty. They were joined by the archers whom the Prophet had commanded to defend the Muslims' rear from attack.

Khalid ibn al-Walid, the commander of the Quraish army, noticed that the Muslim archers had left their positions and launched a sudden attack from the rear. The Muslims were taken by surprise and many were killed or injured. During the confusion the Prophet was left defended by only a handful of Muslims. The Quraish, seeing their chance to kill the Prophet, attacked fiercely and the Prophet was hit in the face and lost some teeth.

The Quraish spread a rumour that the Prophet had been killed and this caused many Muslims to despair. However, on spotting the Prophet, Ka'b ibn Malik called out that the Prophet was still alive. The Muslim army rallied when the news spread. The men gathered round the Prophet to defend him against fresh Quraish attacks. Many Muslims gave their lives defending the Prophet. Abu Dujana shielded him in such a way that he made himself the target of the arrows directed at the Prophet. Ziyad ibn Sakan and seven other devout Companions also lost their lives defending the Prophet.

Eventually, two Muslim archers, Abu Talha and Sa'd, came to the Prophet's rescue. After some confusion the Muslims, led by Abu Bakr, 'Umar, 'Ali and some other

57

Companions, mounted a fierce counter-attack and the Quraish made a hasty retreat. Abu Sufyan fled from the scene expressing joy at the death of many Muslims and saw this as revenge for the Quraish's defeat at Badr.

Some Quraish women behaved like beasts when they mutilated the bodies of the Muslim martyrs. Hind, the wife of Abu Sufyan, ripped open the body of Hamza, the Prophet's uncle, took out his liver and tried to chew it.

When the Muslim women in Madina learned of the Muslim losses, they rushed to the battlefield. Fatima, the Prophet's youngest daughter, tended the Prophet, and dressed his wounds. 'A'isha, Umm Sulaim, Umm 'Umarah and Umm Salt also helped the injured Muslims. Safiyya, Hamza's sister, displayed great courage on learning of her brother's death. Another *Ansari* woman who had lost her father, husband and brother in the battle, still expressed her deepest concern for the Prophet.

The battle was a defeat for the Muslims as, although only a score of disbelievers were killed, seventy Muslims were martyred.

Exercise:

1. Why was the Battle of Uhud fought?
2. Describe the strength of both the Muslim and Quraish armies.
3. How did the hypocrites get their name?
4. What caused the defeat of the Muslim army?
5. What was the name of the leader of the Quraish army?
6. Who dishonoured the body of Hamza?
7. Name the Muslim women who helped the injured?
8. How did the Companions come to the rescue of the Prophet?
9. How many Muslims were martyred in the battle?

The Battles of Bani Qainuqa, Bani Naḍīr and Ahzab

The Prophet had a pact with the Jews of Madina, in which they would help the Muslims to defend the city. They had also agreed to live in peace and friendship. However, instead of keeping their word the Jews plotted against the Muslims and planned to kill the Prophet. When the Quraish attacked Madina the Jews also broke their pact with the Prophet.

The Bani Qainuqa, a leading Jewish tribe, were the first to break their word. While the Muslims were away at the Battle of Badr, the Bani Qainuqa people molested a Muslim woman and killed another Muslim who tried to help her.

On his return from Badr, the Prophet asked the Jews to explain their behaviour. He also tried to bring about peace between the two groups. However, the Jews continued their wicked ways and even declared war against the Muslims. As it was the Bani Qainuqa who had broken the pact, the Prophet led a force of Muslims to their stronghold and besieged them After fifteen days the Bani Qainuqa surrendered and agreed that the Prophet should

59

decide their fate. The Prophet asked them to leave Madina which they did, by migrating to Syria.

The Bani Nadir, another Jewish tribe, also betrayed the Muslims by plotting with the Quraish. They spied on the Muslims and informed the Quraish of their movements. They too plotted to kill the Prophet. When these charges were proved, the Prophet tried to negotiate with the Jews but the hypocrites encouraged them to declare war against the Muslims. The Muslims besieged their forts. After a fortnight they asked the Prophet to allow them to migrate. Carrying their belongings on six hundred camels they left Madina four years after the *Hijra.*

The Battle of Ahzab is also known as 'Ghazwa Khandaq' or the Battle of the Trench. It was an attack on Madina by a joint army of all the leading Arab tribes.

Although the Quraish had killed many Muslims in the Battle of Uhud, they had not won a complete victory. Now, they planned to unite the Arab tribes and launch a joint attack on Madina. The Quraish were also joined by the expelled Bani Nadir. Finally, a huge army of 10,000 soldiers, drawn from all the Arab tribes, set out for Madina.

The Prophet and his Companions, realising they were heavily outnumbered discussed how best they could defend Madina. One of the Companions, Salman al-Farsi, pointed out that Madina could be attacked from one side only, and suggested that they should dig a trench around that side, so that they could defend the town from behind it. The Prophet agreed to this. He and 3,000 Muslims began to dig a trench five feet deep and fifteen feet wide. After three days of hard toil the trench was finished and the Muslims waited patiently to see if it would stop the invading army.

When the large force of Quraish, Jews and other

Arab tribes reached Madina, they were amazed to find the huge trench barring their way. They tried many times to cross the trench but were beaten back by the Muslims. They then decided to lay siege to Madina and to starve the Muslims into surrender. The siege lasted for almost a month, during which time the Muslims suffered great hardships. The weather was very bad and many days they had no food at all. The enemy archers sometimes kept up their attack for hours so that the Muslims did not even have time to offer Prayers. Despite this the Muslims held out.

The Bani Quraiza, the only remaining Jewish tribe in Madina, should have helped the Muslims to defend Madina, according to their pact. Instead, they decided to throw in their lot with the Muslims' enemies, just when the Muslims needed them most. So the Muslims now had an enemy within the city as well as another all around. One of the leaders of the tribes of Aws, Sa'd ibn Mu'adh, was sent to persuade them to stand by their treaty, but the Jewish tribe refused to listen.

The Bani Quraiza were wrong to think that the Muslims were about to be defeated. For Allah helped the Muslims to defeat their enemies. First, as the siege lengthened into weeks, there were disagreements and quarrelling among the enemy. Then, a violent sandstorm that lasted for three days all but destroyed their tents and equipment. Finally, they lost their will to fight, and gave up the siege of Madina and withdrew. The Muslims, though very tired and hungry, were jubilant that they had outlasted and outwitted their enemy's huge army.

As for the Bani Quraiza the Prophet now ordered that their forts should be besieged. After a month the Bani Quraiza laid down their arms and themselves asked that the same Sa'ad ibn Mu'adh should decide their fate. Sa'd decided, in accordance with the Torah, the Jewish Scripture, that all adult males be executed, their women and children held as captives and their property forfeited. In accordance with this judgement 400 of the Bani Quraiza were put to death.

During the Battle of Ahzab and the Battle of Bani Quraiza only ten Muslims lost their lives.

Exercise:

1. What was the original pact between the Muslims and the Bani Qainuqa?
2. How did the Bani Qainuqa break the pact?
3. How were they punished?
4. What were the crimes of the Bani Nadir?
5. How were they punished?
6. Why was it known as the Battle of the Trench?
7. Who were in the enemy camp against the Muslims?
8. How did the trench help the Muslims?
9. What was the fate of the treacherous Bani Quraiza?
10. What was the result of this battle?

LESSON 18

The Hudaibiyya Treaty and the Conquest of Khaybar

The Hudaibiyya Treaty gets its name from Hudaibiyya, a place on the way to Makka, where the treaty was signed.

Six years after the *Hijra* the Prophet and 1,400 Companions set out for Makka to perform *'Umra* (lesser Pilgrimage). This was risky because the Makkan Quraish were still after the blood of the Muslims. But in spite of the dangers the Muslims had rallied round the Prophet and decided to make the Pilgrimage. They were dressed in pilgrims' clothes, had sacrificial camels with them, and carried no arms. But the Quraish decided to prevent the Muslims, at all costs, from performing the Pilgrimage. They asked the neighbouring Arab tribes to help them.

The Muslims broke their journey at Hudaibiyya, where talks were held with the Quraish. First the Quraish sent Budayl, a tribal chief, to them. The Prophet told him that the Muslim party had no plans for war. Although this same message was repeated many times, it had no effect on the Quraish. Finally, 'Uthman ibn Affan was sent to Makka to convince them that the Muslims wanted only to perform the Pilgrimage.

When 'Uthman did not return from Makka, a rumour spread that he had been killed by the Quraish. This would mean a battle. The Muslims then vowed to fight to the death to defend Islam. This oath is known as Bay'at al-Ridwan. The Qur'an praises this oath and those who made it. Since 'Uthman was not present, the Prophet conducted the oath on his behalf.

On learning of the oath and the determination of the Muslims, the Quraish relented. They released 'Uthman and agreed to a ten-year treaty with the Prophet, which contained the following conditions:

1. The Muslims would return to Madina without performing 'Umra.
2. They would visit Makka the next year for Pilgrimage but stay for only three days.
3. On their visit they would not carry arms, except sheathed swords.
4. If any Muslim should flee to Makka, the Quraish would not be bound to return him. However, if any Makkan, even if he was a Muslim, should take shelter in Madina, he would be returned to the Quraish.
5. Arab tribes would be free to enter into a pact with either the Quraish or the Muslims.

The treaty did not seem to contain many benefits for the Muslims but the Qur'an describes it as a 'manifest victory'. Later events proved how the treaty had really been a clear victory for the Muslims. The Muslims had not been free to preach Islam before. Now they could move about freely. As a result, thousands of Arabs embraced Islam which stood for peace and it soon became a strong force.

The Prophet also sent letters to many rulers, calling upon them to accept Islam.

The Negus of Habasha (Abyssinia, now called Ethiopia) was deeply moved by his letter. He replied that he was already a Muslim and that he considered Muhammad to be the Prophet of Allah.

Muqawqis, the ruler of Egypt, showed respect for the Prophet's letter, too. He treated the messenger well and sent him back to the Prophet laden with many gifts although he did not become a Muslim.

Heraclius, the Roman emperor of Byzantium, who had previously heard how Muhammad was respected in his own country as the true Prophet of Allah, believed that Islam would one day also become the religion in his land. However, he was afraid to become a Muslim lest his own people should turn against him.

Chosroes Parvez, the emperor of Persia, tore the letter into pieces. When the Prophet heard what Chosroes had done, he said: 'May Allah tear his kingdom into pieces also.' Chosroes was killed by his own son and his kingdom was destroyed by Allah.

The prosperous town of Khaybar in Arabia was a stronghold of the Jews. It was rich in crops and date groves. The Jews who had been expelled from Madina had taken shelter there. Khaybar had seven fortresses which were manned by 20,000 warriors. The neighbouring tribe, the Ghatfan, were also known for their military strength. The Jews and the Ghatfan joined forces. They looked upon the Muslims as their greatest enemy.

When the Prophet returned from Hudaibiyya, there were skirmishes with the people of Khaybar. The Prophet, deciding to put a stop to this, assembled the Muslim warriors and besieged Khaybar. The siege had continued for about two weeks when one evening the Prophet told his Companions: 'Tomorrow I will appoint the one under whose command Allah will grant us victory.'

The next morning the Prophet entrusted this task to 'Ali. He directed him to offer Islam to the Jews and, if they would not accept, to control them. The Jews refused to embrace Islam, so 'Ali, displaying great bravery, led the attack against the Khaybar fort, until the Jews surrendered. The siege lasted for twenty days, with the deaths of ninety-three Jews and fifteen Muslims.

The Jews pleaded with the Prophet not to expel them from Khaybar. They promised in return to give half of their crops to the Muslims. The Prophet agreed to this. At harvest time Abdullah ibn Rawaha went to Khaybar to receive the share of the crops that had been promised to the Muslims. He asked the Jews to take their share first. This noble gesture was a pleasant surprise for the Jews and they lavished praise on the Muslims for their trustworthiness and justice.

Exercise:

1. Why was the oath known also as Bay'at al-Ridwan?
2. Why were the Muslims at Hudaibiyya?
3. What was 'Uthman's role in the treaty?
4. What were the conditions of the treaty?
5. Why did the terms of the treaty at first cause disappointment among the Muslims?
6. How did the Negus of Abyssinia respond to the Prophet's letter?
7. Why was Heraclius afraid to become a Muslim?
8. Why did Allah destroy the Kingdom of Chosroes?
9. Who inhabited Khaybar?
10. How was it conquered?

LESSON 19

'Umra, the Battle of Muta and the Conquest of Makka

After the Hudaibiyya treaty the Prophet, along with his Companions, could go to Makka to perform *'Umra*. While they were in Makka the non-Muslims left the town. The Prophet stayed for three days performing the rituals of *'Umra*.

Three months after his return to Madina his attention was drawn to some Arab Christian states on the Arabian border with Syria. Shurahbil was the chief of the Busra State. Like other rulers, he had received a letter from the Prophet, inviting him to accept Islam. Instead, he had killed Harith ibn Umayr, who had brought the Prophet's letter to him.

On learning of this, the Prophet despatched an army of 3,000 men to Busra, led by Zayd ibn Haritha. Before the army set out, the Prophet asked them not to kill any hermit, woman or child and not to fell any trees. Shurahbil had an army of 100,000 soldiers, yet the Muslims won the battle. When Zayd was martyred in battle, Ja'far and Abdullah ibn Rawaha took charge. Finally, it was Khalid ibn Walid who took command and brought victory for the

Muslims. The Battle of Muta was the first encounter between Islam and Christianity.

Although the Makkan Quraish were a party to the Hudaibiyya treaty, they soon broke the agreement. The Prophet, therefore, led an army of 10,000 Muslims towards Makka. It was eight years since the *Hijra*. The Makkans were no match for the Muslims and they gave up without a fight. Although the Prophet and his Companions had earlier been persecuted by them, the Prophet allowed the Makkans to go unharmed.

The Prophet then went to the Ka'ba. The non-Muslims had placed hundreds of idols in its compound. He had all these idols destroyed, saying: 'Truth has come and falsehood has vanished. Falsehood, by its nature, is to vanish.' The Ka'ba echoed to this declaration of Allah and the Muslims offered Prayers there. In a speech the Prophet proclaimed the equality of all men, regardless of race or colour.

Exercise:

1. What is *'Umra?*
2. How long did the Prophet stay in Makka performing the Pilgrimage?
3. What led to the Battle of Muta?
4. What instructions did the Prophet give to the Muslim army?
5. Under whose command did the Muslims achieve victory?
6. How many Muslims went to fight and how many were in Shurahbil's army?
7. When and how was Makka conquered?
8. What did the Muslims find in the Ka'ba?

9. How did the Prophet treat those who had been his arch-enemies?
10. What important statements did the Prophet make after the conquest of Makka?

LESSON 20

The Battles of Hunain, Ta'if and Tabuk

Ta'if was the home of the Thaqif tribe. Hunain, a plain between Makka and Ta'if was where the Hawazin tribe lived. Both these tribes, known for their skill in archery, were proud and brave. They deeply resented the Muslim conquest of Makka and they planned to attack the Muslims with a large army. The Prophet, realizing the danger to the Muslims, led an army of 12,000 Muslims to check them.

It was the first time that the Muslims had such a large, well-equipped army. Believing themselves to be a match for anyone, they marched along without watching out for the enemy. Suddenly, they were attacked by the enemy archers, which caused panic in their ranks.

Everyone ran for his life and only the Prophet and a handful of his Companions were left on the main battleground. Displaying great bravery, the Prophet rallied the Muslims and launched a counter-attack and the enemy took to their heels. Thousands were taken prisoner in the Battle of Hunain but the Prophet later set them free.

The Prophet had visited Ta'if eleven years earlier to invite the people to Islam. They had, however, rejected the truth. Members of the Thaqif tribe, who had fled from Hunain, also joined the people of Ta'if. Knowing that they

70

intended to attack the Muslims, the Prophet besieged their fort.

The siege continued for twenty days without either side being able to claim victory in the Battle of Ta'if. The Prophet then prayed to Allah to bring about a change of attitude in the Thaqif. Allah granted his prayer. After some time, a delegation from the Thaqif tribe called on the Prophet, and they eventually embraced Islam.

Shurahbil, whose army had been defeated by the Muslims at the Battle of Muta, planned to take revenge at Tabuk. Realising this, the Prophet told the Muslims to prepare for war. Though it was summer and the Muslims were suffering from the effects of a famine, they responded at once to the Prophet's call.

Abu Bakr gave all that he had to the war fund and 'Uthman also made a generous contribution. An army of 30,000 Muslims was able to set off for Tabuk. At the border, however, news reached them that the enemy had already fled. The Prophet, not wanting the journey to be wasted, entered into an alliance with several tribes of the area who pledged their allegiance to the Islamic state.

Exercise:

1. What was the initial setback for the Muslims?
2. Describe the result of the Battle of Hunain.
3. What happened to the prisoners?
4. Why did the Prophet go to Ta'if?
5. What is a siege?
6. How were the people of Ta'if won over to Islam?
7. What caused the Battle of Tabuk?
8. Who helped to fund the army?
9. Why was there no fighting?
10. What did the Prophet do to save a wasted journey?

LESSON 21

The End of the Prophet's Life

In the tenth year after the *Hijra,* the Prophet went to Makka to perform *Hajj.* From miles around people flocked to Makka, wanting to be led in the Pilgrimage by the Prophet himself. For the first time in hundreds of years the true meaning was given to the *Hajj.* This time there were no idolaters but 125,000 Muslims were present. Only the rites according to Islam were performed.

The Prophet said many times that the Ka'ba was built by Ibrahim, *alayhis-salam,* and that the rites Ibrahim established should be observed by the Muslims from now on.

It was a part of the Pilgrimage to go to 'Arafah, a valley about thirteen miles from Makka on the road to Ta'if. A hill in the valley is called Jabal al-Rahma; it means the 'Mount of Mercy'. There the Prophet stood and delivered what is known as his Farewell Sermon. He began with the words: 'I do not know if I shall ever meet you in this place after this time.'

In the sermon he said: 'Glory be to Allah who alone deserves all praise. O people! You should not associate anyone with Him. Nor should you commit manslaughter or fornication. You should not steal. There is no prophet after me. You should be careful about performing all religious duties. The life, blood, honour and property of a Muslim are sacred for another. You should not indulge in any excess. Nor should you deviate from your faith. All Muslims are brothers in faith. You have a heavy responsibility regarding women. You should treat them well. Fighting in Allah's cause is the supreme worship. You should adhere to the Book of Allah.'

The Prophet asked the people if they would bear witness that he had truly and faithfully delivered Allah's message to them. They all declared loudly that they would.

Also at this time was revealed the verse of the Qur'an: 'This day I have perfected for you your religion and completed My favour to you. And it is My will to choose Islam for you as your religion' (5: 3).

Shortly afterwards, in Madina, the Prophet knew from Allah that his death was near. Now that Allah had assured him his mission was fulfilled, he would not choose to linger in this world. He suffered from severe headaches but even when his illness worsened he continued to lead the Prayers in the Mosque and to support his followers in their *Jihad* for the sake of Allah. One day he was not able to go to the Mosque to lead the Prayers. He sent orders that Abu Bakr should take his place. Abu Bakr was the closest to the Prophet of all his Companions, and he led the Prayers during the Prophet's illness.

Then on the twelfth day of the month of Rabi' al-Awwal, in the year 11 H, the Prophet appeared in the Mosque, even though he was weak from his illness. The Prayer had already begun when he entered, but the whole congregation stopped their Prayer until he signalled for them to continue. Abu Bakr continued to pray but stepped back, to allow the Prophet to take the place of the *Imam*.

73

But the Prophet gently pushed him forward again and prayed sitting down, slightly to the right of Abu Bakr.

Everyone saw how the Prophet gave his place to Abu Bakr. Some of the people believed that he had recovered. He had made a great effort to answer the call to Prayer. He wanted to give heart to his Companions, to support them in the coming *Jihad* in Syria, and to show his support for Abu Bakr.

When, later that day, the Prophet died in his home, in the arms of his wife 'A'isha, the people were not ready to believe it. Even 'Umar refused to believe the news. But Abu Bakr, after he had seen the body of the Prophet and spoken over it his words of sorrow and love, came out to the people and calmed them down.

He recited to them the words of the Qur'an which Allah had given to the Prophet after the defeat at Uhud: 'Muhammad is but a messenger, and messengers have passed away before him. If he dies or is killed, will you turn your heels (run away from your responsibilities as Muslims)? Whoever does so will not thereby hurt Allah. And Allah will reward those who give thanks.'

From the very beginning of the world Prophets had been inviting people to live in total surrender to Allah, their Creator. Among the long chain of Prophets which concluded with the Prophet Muhammad were Nuh (Noah), Ibrahim (Abraham), Musa (Moses), Dawud (David), Sulaiman (Soloman), and 'Isa (Jesus).

The Prophet Muhammad was buried in the place where he died. 'Ali and the Companions looked after the funeral arrangements. Abu Bakr was chosen by the Companions to be the leader of the Muslims and he accepted the duties of Caliph. When he did so, he said to the people: 'If I do well, help me; and if I do wrong, set me right.'

Exercise:

1. How many years after the *Hijra* did the Prophet go to Makka for *Hajj*?
2. How many Muslims accompanied him?
3. Where did the Prophet deliver his Farewell Sermon?
4. What were the main points of the Farewell Sermon?
5. Which verse of the Qur'an did Allah reveal that same day?
6. Describe the Prophet's illness and his strength of character to cope with it.
7. Describe his death and the reactions of those who loved him.
8. Where was the Prophet buried?
9. Name some of the Prophets who came before him.
10. What did Abu Bakr say when he accepted the duties of Caliph?

LESSON 22

The Prophet's Family

Khadija was the first wife of the Prophet Muhammad. After Khadija's death, the Prophet married 'A'isha, the daughter of Abu Bakr Siddiq and Sauda bint Zam'ah. Later on, he married Zainab bint Khuzaima, Umm Salma, Zainab bint Jahsh, Juwairya, Umm Habiba bint Abu Sufyan, Hafsa, the daughter of 'Umar ibn al-Khattab, Maimuna bint al-Harith and Safiyya bint Huyay ibn Akhtab.

At the time of the Prophet's death all his wives, except Khadija and Zainab bint Khuzaima, were still alive and they undertook the task of guiding the Companions and other Muslims. The Prophet also married Mariya, a Coptic slave girl from Egypt. Each of the Prophet's wives were given the title of Umm al-Mu'minin, 'Mother of the Believers', and no Muslim was permitted to marry them. May Allah be pleased with them.

All the Prophet's children, except Ibrahim, were by his first wife, Khadija. Two sons, al-Qasim, and Abd-Allah died in infancy. Mariya the Copt bore a son, Ibrahim, who also died in infancy. The Prophet's four daughters survived and were blessed with Islam. His eldest daughter, Zainab, was married to Abu al-'As. She passed away in 8 H, leaving a daughter, Umama.

The Prophet's second daughter, Ruqayya, was married to 'Uthman, after he had embraced Islam. She passed away in Madina in 2 H. Umm Kulthum, the third daughter, was married to 'Uthman after Ruqayya's death. She passed away in 9 H. The Prophet's beloved youngest daughter, Fatima, was married to 'Ali. She bore him two sons: Hasan and Husain. May Allah be pleased with them all.

Exercise:

1. Who was the Prophet's first wife?
2. Who was 'A'isha?
3. Name all the Prophet's wives.
4. How many children were born to Khadija?
5. What was the name of the Prophet's eldest daughter?
6. What was the name of the Prophet's youngest daughter?
7. Which of the first Muslims did his youngest daughter marry?
8. What were the names of the Prophet's two grand-sons?
9. What name was given to each of the Prophet's wives?
10. When the Prophet passed away, how many of his children were still living?

LESSON 23

The Prophet's Good Deeds

When someone asked 'A'isha about the conduct of the Prophet, she said that his actions mirrored the Qur'an. All that the Qur'an preaches could be seen in his conduct. The Qur'an itself testifies that the Prophet's conduct was the best.

The Prophet was very modest, warm-hearted, helpful and merciful. He loved the low and the high alike, and was generous to everyone. He helped others whenever he could. He never hurt anyone. He often provided food while remaining hungry himself. Once, when a Companion married and had no food for the wedding feast, the Prophet told him to ask his wife 'A'isha for some flour. Apart from that small quantity of flour, there was no other food in the Prophet's house.

The Prophet was so generous and indifferent to riches that he would not save money. He was content only after he had given away his money. Once, the chief of Fidak sent him four camel-loads of grain. The Prophet sold the grain in order to repay a debt, and had some money left. He refused to go home until he had given it all away. He spent the night in the Mosque and went home only when he was sure that all the money had been given to the poor.

The Prophet was also very hospitable. He enter-tained both Muslims and non-Muslims at his house, where he personally served them and looked after their needs. Often he gave a guest all the food in the house while he and his family went hungry. Once, an unbeliever came to the Prophet's house as a guest. The Prophet served him with the milk of a goat, and the guest drank all the milk. Then, although the guest drank the milk of six more goats, the Prophet continued to serve him.

The Prophet got up during the night to attend to the needs of his guests. When he was at home, he helped with the housework. He mended his own clothes and shoes and milked the goats. When the Muslims were building the Prophet's Mosque and digging the ditch at Madina, he worked equally hard alongside them. The Prophet had a special place in his heart for orphans. He constantly urged his Companions to behave well towards them. He said that the best house is the one in which an orphan is properly cared for, and the worst house is the one in which an orphan is ill-treated.

The Prophet treated the poor in such a way that they did not feel humiliated. He helped and consoled them. Often he prayed that he should die destitute and be treated with the destitute on the Last Day. Once, a tribe called on him who were so poor that they were without shoes, bare-headed and scantily clad. The Prophet was very disturbed by their plight and asked the Companions to help them.

The Prophet always helped the oppressed to get justice. He was merciful towards the weak and assisted the needy. He let it be known that if a Muslim died and left behind a debt, he would repay it. He took no share from the inheritance of the deceased person as that belonged to the descendants.

The Prophet visited and cared for the sick, whatever their faith. He pardoned the guilty and prayed for the well-being even of his enemies. He spoke good of those who were out to do him harm, and he did not take revenge even against those who wanted to kill him. Once, a person who intended to kill him was arrested by the Companions and brought before him. The man was afraid that the Prophet would harm him, but the Prophet told him not to fear and said: 'Had you wanted to kill me, you could not have done so.'

The Prophet took good care of his neighbours. He sent them gifts and urged his Companions to follow his example. In a gathering, his Companions once heard him remark: 'By Allah, he would not be a believer! By Allah, he would not be a believer!' A Companion asked: 'What do you mean, O Prophet of God?' He said: 'I mean the one whose neighbour is not safe from his mischief.' When a slave-girl of Madina asked for his help with some matter, he obliged her at once.

Exercise:

1. Why was there often no food in the Prophet's house?
2. Give examples to show the Prophet's lack of interest in money.
3. Give examples of the Prophet's hospitality.
4. What jobs did he undertake?
5. Why was he particularly interested in orphans?
6. Why did he want to be poor when he died?
7. How did he help Muslims who died in debt?
8. How did he treat his enemies?
9. Did he care for sick people who were not Muslims? What did he do for them?
10. How did he treat his neighbours?

LESSON 24

The Prophet's Character

The Prophet had a special love for children. He caressed and kissed them. He gave fruit to the youngest ones. He always greeted the children whom he met on his way.

In the time before Islam, women were ill-treated. But the Prophet granted them their rights and through his own example he showed that they should be treated with respect. As the male Companions always thronged around the Prophet, the women were often unable to hear him. So, at the women's request, he reserved a day especially for them. They asked him questions freely and frankly, and the Prophet always tried to help them.

The Prophet was sent as a mercy for the whole of mankind. He disapproved of excess and injustice in any form. He did not like animals to be mistreated. Once, when someone took an egg from a bird's nest, the bird became very disturbed. When the Prophet saw what had happened, he told the person to replace the egg in the nest.

In the Prophet's eyes the rich and the poor were equal. A woman who belonged to the Makhzum tribe was charged with theft. Members of the tribe asked Usama, the Prophet's favourite Companion, to plead on her behalf. The Prophet told him that earlier communities had been destroyed because no action had been taken against the nobles when they did wrong but the weak were punished. He said: 'By Allah! Had my own daughter Fatima stolen something, her hands would have been cut off.'

It is recorded that Anas said that he spent ten years in the company of the Prophet as his servant. During that time, however, he was never criticised or beaten by the Prophet. The Prophet never questioned anything he did, or anything he had failed to do.

The Prophet never beat anyone in his whole life. Although he led the Muslims into battle many times, he himself never attacked his enemies. In the Battle of Uhud he was constantly stoned and hit several times by arrows, but he stood his ground and did not strike back at the enemy.

In the Battle of Hunain many of the Muslim warriors had begun to retreat when the enemy had taken them by surprise, but the Prophet stood his ground and the Muslims then returned to fight and won the battle. The Companions reported that in battle the Prophet took up a position which was avoided by even the bravest Muslim. In the Battle of Uhud, though he received a head injury and lost some teeth, the Prophet continued to pray that Allah would pardon his enemies.

The Prophet was never down-hearted, though he sometimes faced failure in the early years of his mission. When they were being repeatedly persecuted by the disbelievers in Makka, the Companions asked the Prophet why he did not pray for the destruction of their enemies. The Prophet who was sad to be asked this question said: 'Those who believed before you were mutilated. Their bodies were cut into pieces by iron saws and their flesh torn apart. However, even this torture could not turn them from the truth. By Allah! Islam will one day reign supreme.

The day is not very far off when a traveller will go from Sana to Hadreamaut without fear. He will be filled with only the fear of Allah.

The Prophet once told his uncle that he would not give up preaching the truth even if the unbelieving Quraish placed the sun and the moon on his right hand and left hand.

One day, the Prophet was alone in the Muslim camp close to the battleground. He lay down to rest in the shade of a tree and fell asleep. One of the enemy came along by chance and, seeing the Prophet alone and asleep he quietly removed the Prophet's sword from its sheath and raised it over him. Then, as the Prophet awoke, he said: 'O Muhammad! Who can deliver you from me now?' The Prophet calmly replied: 'Allah.' Hearing the Prophet's reply, the man trembled with fear and fainted. The Prophet disarmed him and when he came to asked him the same question. The man had no answer. The Prophet let the man go.

Exercise:

1. Describe what the Prophet did when he met children.
2. How did the Prophet improve conditions for women?
3. How do we know that the Prophet cared about birds and animals?
4. How did the Prophet say his daughter would have been treated if she had stolen something?
5. Did the Prophet ever attack anyone?
6. Give an example of the Prophet's bravery in battle.

7. The Prophet said there was only one thing to be frightened of. What was it?
8. What gifts could not have persuaded the Prophet to give up preaching Islam?
9. Describe how an enemy found an opportunity to kill the Prophet.
10. How did the Prophet disarm this enemy?

LESSON 25

The Prophet's Trustworthiness

Though they collected booty from their battles, the Muslims did not become wealthy. Nor was there any change in the Prophet's lifestyle. He did not begin living a life of comfort and luxury. Whatever was in the Prophet's house was always shared out among the needy and the destitute. The Prophet used to say that a piece of cloth for covering the body and dry bread is sufficient for anyone. According to 'A'isha, the Prophet had only one set of clothes.

Often there was no food in the Prophet's house. He would not eat dinner for several days. Sometimes months would pass when food was not prepared every day in his kitchen. Often he only had dates to eat. Sometimes the Companions sent him milk, but 'A'ishah reported that the Prophet did not have a proper meal during the time he was in Madina.

Once, a hungry man came to the Prophet's house and asked for food. He sent him to one of his wives. However, there was no food there. He sent him to another wife, but again there was no food. The same thing happened with all the Prophet's wives. None of them had any food. They could only offer water to the hungry man.

One day, the Prophet left his house at noon without having had any food. He then met Abu Bakr and 'Uthman who also had not eaten that day. The Prophet then went to Abu Ayyub al-Ansari's house who, when he saw the Prophet ran to meet him and offered him a bunch of dates. He also prepared a meal for the Prophet. The Prophet ate a little food and then asked Abu Ayyub al-Ansari to send some food to his daughter Fatima who had not had anything to eat for days.

The Prophet was very fond of his daughter Fatima. However, he never gave her anything of value such as ornaments or property. Fatima herself attended to the household chores. She fetched water and baked bread. Once, when she asked the Prophet to get a slave to help in the house, the Prophet told her to recite a special prayer instead. At one time, several boy and girl slaves were presented to the Prophet and Fatima asked him to give her one of the slaves. The Prophet told her that other destitute Muslims were more deserving than her.

The Prophet did not like to be in debt to others. Even at the time of his migration from Makka, when Abu Bakr presented him with a camel for the journey he paid him for the camel. If he accepted a gift from someone, he always gave a gift in return. The Prophet was always very fair in his dealings. He used to say that the best person is the one who repays his debt quickly. Once, when he borrowed a camel, he returned a better camel. Also, when he misplaced a pot which he had borrowed, he paid the owner for the pot.

The Prophet always kept his word. He never betrayed anyone. One of the clauses of the Hudaibiyya Treaty was that a Makkan Muslim would be sent back to the Makkans if they asked for his return. When Abu Jandal, a Makkan Muslim migrated to Madina, he pleaded with the Prophet not to return him to the unbelieving Makkans. The Muslims were very disturbed by Abu Jandal's plight, but the Prophet told him: 'O Abu Jandal! Have patience, I cannot break my word. Allah will certainly find a way for you.'

The Prophet always told the truth. This was even acknowledged by his worst enemies. Abu Jahl said: 'O Muhammad! I do not hold you to be a liar, although I do not believe in what you preach.'

Exercise:

1. What did the Prophet say were sufficient possessions for anyone?
2. Give examples of the shortage of food in the Prophet's home.
3. Describe the Prophet's generosity when Abu Ayyub Ansari offered him food.
4. Why would the Prophet not let his daughter have a slave to help her with the housework?
5. What did the Prophet do when he received a gift?
6. What did the Prophet do after borrowing a camel?
7. Did the Prophet always keep his word?
8. Give an example of how the Prophet kept his word even when a Muslim was in distress.
9. How did the Prophet say the Muslim in distress would get help?
10. Give an example of how one of the Prophet's worst enemies admitted that the Prophet always told the truth.

LESSON 26

The Prophet's Humility

The Prophet was very modest and shy. If he was offended by someone's remarks in a gathering he remained silent. His displeasure showed only on his face. Once he had made up his mind, he used to get things done as he had decided. Before the Battle of Uhud, he consulted the Companions, who agreed that they should fight the enemy. However, when the Prophet returned dressed ready for battle, they asked him to reverse the decision. The Prophet refused, saying that a Prophet does not change his mind.

The Prophet was very brave. Once, there was a rumour in Madina that the enemy was about to attack the town. Though everyone rushed to prepare for battle, the Prophet was the first to come out and look for the enemy. He was never afraid of danger.

Simplicity was another feature of the Prophet's character. In his habits, dress and lifestyle, he never sought luxury and comfort. He took whatever was offered to him. He wore whatever simple clothes were available. Once, he went to 'A'isha's house and found some ornamental work on the ceiling. He tore it down at once and told her that Allah had not given wealth for ornamentation. Once, when he noticed that Fatima was wearing a gold necklace, he said to her: 'Will you not feel bad if someone says that there is a necklace of fire around the neck of the Prophet's daughter?'

Some of the Companions used to devote the greater part of their time to prayers and other acts of worship. In doing this, they sometimes neglected their family duties. The Prophet discouraged this. Once, he was told that Abdullah ibn 'Umar had vowed to fast and to pray throughout the night. When Ibn 'Umar confirmed that this was his intention, the Prophet told him to remember that he had certain obligations to his wives and family, as well as to his own body.

When calling upon someone, the Prophet was very careful not to stand directly in front of the door. He stood to the side of the door so that he could not see into the house.

The Prophet was very particular about cleanliness. Once, when he saw someone dressed in dirty clothes, he asked him to improve his appearance.

When speaking he often paused so that others could follow him. He never interrupted anyone. He simply ignored offensive remarks. Most of the time he remained silent. He used to talk only about important matters. Although he would often smile, he never laughed.

The Prophet was ever-conscious of Allah and always tried to please Him. He always remembered Allah while in the company of his Companions or wives. He used to rise immediately on hearing the call for Prayer. He spent most of the night in prayers. Sometimes he prayed throughout the night and recited long verses from the Qur'an. Once, he said in a very moving manner: 'O Children of Abd Manaf! I cannot save you against Allah. O Abbas, son of 'Abd al-Muttalib, O Safiyya, O Fatima, I cannot save any of you from Allah.'

A Companion reported that he once visited the Prophet and found him so engrossed in prayer that he was sobbing loudly. Once, when the Prophet visited a grave he started weeping. He wept so much that the soil was moistened. He always urged others to live the kind of life that would assure them of entry to Heaven.

The Prophet's character and conduct were intended to be an example for all Muslims at all times. We should strive to live as he lived, for that is the only way to gain Allah's pleasure.

Exercise:

1. How did the Prophet show his displeasure when someone offended him?
2. Give examples of how we know the Prophet scorned luxuries.
3. Did the Prophet think family duties were important?
4. How did the Prophet show respect for privacy when visiting?
5. How did the Prophet show consideration for listeners when he was speaking?
6. What did the Prophet do when he heard the call to Prayer?
7. Did the Prophet constantly remember Allah? Give reasons for your answer.
8. Why did the Prophet sob when he was praying?
9. Why did the Prophet sob at a grave he was visiting?
10. Why should we strive to live as the Prophet lived?

The Prophet's Companions Recall His Qualities

The character of the Prophet as remembered by his Companions, *radi Allahu 'anhum:*

Anas ibn Malik said that the Prophet Muhammad was of medium build and had a noble bearing. He had slightly curly hair and a fair complexion.

Ibrahim ibn Muhammad ibn Ali ibn Abi Talib said that the Prophet was more liberal-minded than most men. He was gentle by nature and always spoke the truth. He was always very courteous to others. Those who came to know him soon grew to love and respect him.

Hasan ibn 'Ali, the grandson of the Prophet, said that he asked his uncle, Hind ibn Abu Hala about the Prophet's appearance and behaviour. Hind ibn Abu Hala told him that the Prophet was of medium height, he walked softly but firmly and leaning slightly forward. His eyes were usually directed more towards the ground than to the sky, but he looked straight at a thing with a firm gaze. He made his Companions walk in front of him and was the first to greet another Muslim.

Jabir ibn Samura said: 'The Prophet of Allah had a wide mouth. His eyes were of light brown hue and his

91

heels had little flesh. I saw the Prophet on a moonlit night. He had a red cloak over his body and I looked attentively in turn towards him and the moon. He certainly appeared to me to be more beautiful than the moon itself.'

Sa'id al-Jurayri related that he heard Abu Tufayl saying that he had seen the Prophet of Allah. When Sa'id asked him about the Prophet's appearance, he replied that the Prophet had a fair complexion, was handsome and had a moderate temper.

Abu Bakr said to the Prophet that it was strange that he appeared older than he really was. The Prophet replied that some verses in the Qur'an described the Day of Resurrection and, because of his anxiety about the fate of mankind, this had made him appear older.

Abu Sa'id al-Khudri said that when the Prophet of Allah wore a new garment he would praise Allah Who had given him the garment and pray also for the purity of the clothes.

Samura ibn Jundub related that the Prophet said: 'Wear white clothes; verily they are very pure and clean; and shroud your dead in white.'

Abu Hurayra narrated that the Prophet said: 'When anyone amongst you puts on shoes, he should begin with the right foot. When he removes his shoes, he should start with the left one so that the right one is last.'

'A'isha said that in his personal habits, such as combing his hair, putting on his shoes and performing ablutions, the Prophet would always begin from the right.

Abu Hurayra said that he had never seen anything more beautiful than the Prophet. The sun seemed to shine from his face and he walked so quickly that the Companions sometimes could not keep up with him.

Ibrahim ibn Muhammad, a descendant of 'Ali ibn

Abi Talib, said that when 'Ali described the Prophet, he used to say that he walked as if he were going down a hill.

Abdur Rahman ibn Abu Bakr narrated, on the authority of his father, that the Prophet asked whether he would inform them about the greatest sins. The Prophet said that the worst sins were setting up rivals to Allah and disobedience to parents. He also said that not to tell the truth was also one of the greatest sins.

Exercise:

1. Describe some of the Prophet's features.
2. What did Hind ibn Abu Hala tell Hasan ibn 'Ali about the Prophet's appearance?
3. What did Jabir ibn Samura say about the Prophet's appearance?
4. Who told the Prophet that he looked older than he really was?
5. What was the Prophet's answer?
6. What did the Prophet do when he wore a new garment?
7. Why is it good for Muslims to wear white?
8. What was the Prophet's habit when putting on and taking off his shoes?
9. What was the Prophet's manner of walking?
10. What did the Prophet say were the greatest sins?

The Prophet's Companions Recall His Actions

Abu Ayyub al-Ansari said that one day they were in the company of the Prophet when food was placed before him. There was a great blessing on the food which they ate first but less blessing on the food which they ate last. When the Prophet was asked why this was so, he replied that they had praised Allah before they began to eat but, when later someone sat down and began to eat without praising Allah, then Satan ate with him.

'A'isha narrated that the Prophet said that if a Muslim forgets to say *'Bismillah'* (In the Name of Allah) before beginning to eat, then, when he remembers, he should repeat the name of Allah by saying: 'Let it be in the name of Allah at its beginning and at its end.'

'Umar ibn Abi Salma related that the Prophet said: 'Come near, O child! Mention the name of God and eat with the right hand and eat from the side that is near you.'

Abu Sa'id al-Khudri said that the Prophet, when he had finished eating, used to say: 'All praise is due to Allah who has fed us and given us drink and made us Muslims.'

Anas ibn Malik said: 'Verily Allah is pleased with those who eat a morsel and drink a sip and praise Him for it.'

It was related that the Prophet said: 'If any one of you is given a fragrant flower he should not refuse it because flowers come from Paradise.'

'A'isha said that the Prophet spoke slowly and distinctly, pronouncing every word separately so that those who heard him would remember his words.

Hind ibn Abu Hala said that the Prophet usually remained silent. He spoke only when necessary. He spoke slowly and clearly. He spoke to enjoin righteousness or to condemn wrongdoing. He did not indulge in idle talk. He never spoke unjustly of anyone, nor would he allow others to do so. The things in this world could not annoy him but, when truth was disregarded, he became very passionate. He did not take offence at any remark of a personal nature, nor did he seek to revenge himself upon anyone. He looked away when he was angry.

Abu Hurayra narrated that the Prophet said that the best words which the Arab poets had chanted were the lines of Labid, beginning: 'Beware! Everything except Allah is perishable.'

Al-Bara ibn Azib narrated that when the Prophet lay down on his bed he put his right palm below his right cheek and said: 'O Allah! Save me from the punishment on the day when You will raise Your creatures.'

When the Prophet went to bed he said: 'O Allah! In Your name I lie down and in Your name I arise'; and when he awoke he said: 'All praise to Allah Who has revived us after we were made to die and unto Him shall be the Resurrection.'

'A'isha said that every night when the Prophet went to bed he would place his palms together, blow upon them and read the following Suras: *Qulhuwa' llahu Ahad, Qul A'udhu bi Rabbi'l-Falaq* and *Qul A'udhu bi Rabbi'n-*

Nas of the Qur'an. Then he would rub his hands over his body as far as he could, beginning with his head and face and the front of his body.

Someone asked Umm Salama about the way the Prophet read the Qur'an. She said that he read the Qur'an very clearly, pronouncing every word distinctly.

Ibn 'Abbas said that when the Prophet read the Qur'an in his room he could be heard clearly in the courtyard below.

Anas ibn Malik narrated that the Prophet used to visit the sick, attend funerals, travel by donkey and accept even the invitations of slaves.

Husain related that his father said that when the Prophet stayed at his house, he divided his time into three parts. He kept one part for Allah, another for his family and the remaining part for himself. He divided his own part between himself and the people.

The Prophet said: 'Bring to me the needs of those persons who are not able to bring them to me; for the feet of that person who conveys the needs of persons who are unable to come to a leader themselves, will be firm on the Day of Resurrection.'

Husain related that his father said that the Prophet invoked the name of Allah when he sat down and when he stood up.

Anas ibn Malik said that the Prophet never asked: 'Why did you do that?' nor did he appear to criticize anyone by asking: 'Why didn't you do it?' The Prophet was the best of men in politeness and manners.

'A'isha said that the Prophet never returned evil for evil; he would forgive and pardon.

Anas ibn Malik said that the Prophet did not keep anything for himself for the next day.

Exercise:

1. What did the Prophet say a Muslim should do if he forgot to praise Allah before eating?
2. What did the Prophet say when he finished eating?
3. What words did the Prophet say when he went to bed and when he woke up?
4. Which Suras of the Qur'an did the Prophet recite every night?
5. Describe how the Prophet read the Qur'an.
6. Why did the Prophet visit the sick and accept the invitation of slaves?
7. What did the Prophet say when he sat down and when he stood up?
8. Did the Prophet ever personally criticize anyone?
9. What does it mean to say the Prophet never returned evil for evil?
10. Why did the Prophet prefer to forgive?

Glossary

Ahad	Allah is One.
Amin	Describing a trustworthy person.
Ansar	A helper.
Bismillah	In the name of Allah.
Hadith	A saying of the Prophet.
Hajj	Pilgrimage to the Ka'ba in Makka during the month of Dhu ul-Hijja.
Hijra	The emigration of Muslims from Makka to Madina.
Imam	The person who leads Muslims in prayers, originally performed by the leader of the Muslim state or his deputy.
Jihad	To try one's utmost to establish the Islamic system: a struggle in the way of Allah to seek His pleasure.
jinn	Creatures created from fire by Allah before He created mankind. Normally invisible, they wander at will on earth.
Khutba	A sermon.
La-ilaha-Illa-Allah	There is no god but ALLAH.
Mu'adhdhin	The caller of the *Adhan* inviting Muslims to Prayers.
Muhajirun	Emigrants.
Sadiq	Describing a strictly honest person.
'Umra	Lesser Pilgrimage to the Ka'ba in Makka.

98

The Middle East during the
Life of the Prophet Muhammad

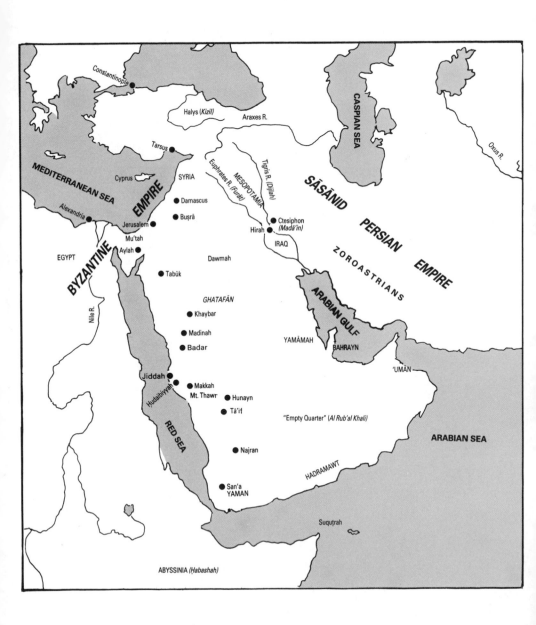

NOTES

NOTES

NOTES